You At Your Best

You At Your Best

LIFE'S OPPORTUNITIES ARE LIMITLESS

Kare F. Green

To order additional copies of this book, contact:
Xlibris Corporation
1-888-795-4274
www.Xlibris.com
Orders@Xlibris.com
58124

Contents

Acknowledgements

I would like to thank God the Lord Jesus first and foremost, my husband Shaun Green, my daughter and son Shaunice & Shaun-Joseph Green, my mother Valerie Rogers, my mother-in law Giselle Green, my brothers' Jason & Jeremiah, my friends Nyiesha Campbell & Eva, my colleagues Alicia Joo MSED & Michael Johnson MSED, my past field supervisor Valerie Lyons MSED CRC LMH, my attorneys & friends Stuart Shestack & Jamie Levy, & to Everyone that inspired this book.

Preface

This book takes you the reader into a realm of self we all need to visit and revisit throughout our lives. Our daily feelings and focus are directly connected to how far we make it in life. There are many clichés that we hear and they lose their effect. None the less, I have to say it, you can achieve anything you put your mind to, and I am a living testament of that notion. There are many people that are an example of what the definition of determination is and the concept mind over matter.

One person I truly admire is Oprah Winfrey and I must say I am very selective about who I consider a person of importance. For instance, yes she is a symbol of wealth, power, and respect just from the mere mention of her name. However, more importantly she worked and strived to reach where she is now, a fighter, a person giving back to people, a person seemingly at her best and that is what this book is about. It is about motivating YOU the reader in order to motivate others, and than we all are inspired to becoming what we really want to be at our Best.

You make it possible for yourself to make an impact in the world. You at your best the book is also about empowerment, and it is about spreading positivity and strength.

How to use this book

There are so many people that have to rise above the cards that life dealt them. Now begin to commit to yourself by planning your success and enjoying this motivational book! It is suggested that you the reader read the quotes before you start your day. Read the quotes out loud and then again silently. Begin reading this book preferably at the beginning of a month. There are pages to fill out in the back of the book. You can write your short term goals, long term goals, write your plan, steps, and dates of your desired goals.

Therefore, you can personalize the literature. This is your book. Internalize the quotes and live the life you truly deserve! At your best you're constructive & productive.

At Your Best,

- *What are you grateful for today and remember the day will be in tune with the rhythm of your spirit, be positive, you get what you put out*

At Your Best,

- *Everyday focus on the things you want, do not focus on the things that are lacking, put everything in perspective, and in its necessary place in your life for your expected desired results*

At Your Best,

- *The sun is out give someone a million dollar smile because they're in the presence of greatness they may not know it yet, but we are all great. now tap into that greatness.*

At Your Best,

- *Success can be a minuscule achievement Today be productive not just busy, every little step towards achievement is a giant step in the right direction*

At Your Best,

- *Our success is a journey embrace the travel time, many would like to be an overnight success which is not usually the case so enjoy the time making it happen*

At Your Best,

- *Keep good relations with good people
  call someone dear to you today, just take
  a minute out of your busy day, always
  remember to validate your care for those
  that matter even buisness partners*

At Your Best,

- *The mind is our capital, so as human intellects we must reign our country because once imperialized the vision is captured*

At Your Best,

- *The thought today is do you truly know
  yourself and are you true to your purpose
  of existence, it is all apart of the healthy
  positive mindset being in tune with self*

At Your Best,

- *There is only one option to go forward not backwards, progression not stagnation, there is a time to stay still yet you are still moving forward if that's the neccesary choice*

At Your Best,

- *You are special and stand out from the rest, give someone the pleasure of seeing your individuality today, it is not always about the commonality in people but the unique factors that will allow you to separate and coin your wealth*

At Your Best,

- *Remember to walk with purpose, enjoy the process of acceleration, look good, by exuding a positive attitude into the atmosphere*

At Your Best,

- *We focus our energy on the things we want
  Brain power is a strong powerful tool Use
  it effectively and we will see results*

At Your Best,

- *You may feel like a trout going upstream,*
- *But remember all your work will pay off,*
- *You will reap the benefits, manifest, and give birth to your ambitions*

At Your Best,

- *There is a cause and effect to everything*
  In life even if we choose to not choose, so
  What will we choose today that will cause
  A change to work in our favor

At Your Best,

- *Prioritize don't get set off track, there*
  Will always be distractions, who you truly
  Are is determined when no one is around,
  In the trenches of life, so stride in integrity

At Your Best,

- *The true value of life is the freedom of time, peace of mind, making memories with love ones, and knowing your purpose for your life at your best and what it would truly mean for you to achieve at your highest potential*

At Your Best,

- *There are thousands of choices through out one's life, but one choice that will set you apart and determine whether you will be on top or not is your choice to never give up*

At Your Best,

Life, what is the true meaning,
Is it knowing how to balance
the ups and downs,
Is it living in the mountains
with less people,
Is it living the corporate nine to five
life with a couple of vacation days,
Or is it just being and finding the medium,
Go figure but remember to embrace the joys

At Your Best,

- *You are what you read and think, you set the standards already in your head of what you are going to accomplish and your proceedings confirm or negate the outcome*

At Your Best,

- *Do you feel like you're at a good place in your life, if not, march in your destiny, if you are at a great place continue to live in the true meaning of life which is freedom*

At Your Best,

- *It is very simple failing is not the issue in
  life that determines success It is moving
  past the concept or idea of not succeeding
  that truly determines one's latter state.*

At Your Best,

- *What differentiates you from average is your decision to live out your dreams no matter what obstacles come and putting your goals and dreams into real view by taking action*

At Your Best,

- *Stay in good spirits today, deadlines might be due, this might not be a good day or week, but you never know who is going to help you so help another person by being in a good state of mind, life can be a whirl wind at times but stay in peace*

At Your Best,

- *Everything is work,*
- *So use the power of choice wisely and effectively,*
  There is a fatal decision and that is to stop working,
  Every path has an end, what is the end of yours

At Your Best,

- *We write the story of our life, what do you want to write on the page today for your book, everyday is a live narrative of a voyage, where are you going and what is your quest*

At Your Best,

-   *Whatever you put your mind to do is
    what you will do,
    No one chooses where
    we work, and want to become,
    No one but us
    There may be life pressures and influences
    But at the end of the day it's your life*

At Your Best,

- *If you are reading this quote for the day then you should be close to the catalyst of your written preparation, speak your goals into existence, visualize them, paint a picture of them, and walk in the steps of your plan*

At Your Best,

- *With all the self-assurance, force, and Self driven power inside of you remember There are expected trials and uncertainties, we do know that life is full of the unexpected, we cannot predict the Future, but do not let that stop the process of your success*

At Your Best,

- *Are you ready to conquer the world, are you ready to believe in yourself, are you Ready to fail, are you ready to succeed, are you ready to be self fulfilled, can you accept success and actually living the reality of life above middle America*

At Your Best,

- *We are the masters of our fate, period, we decide what our reality will be, we focus a lot on external factors as a contribution To our reason for being, yet at times we must embrace self atonomy, breeth, enjoy the gift of life, close your eyes for a moment*
Do you see it

At Your Best,

- *The best thing today is you, your very Life touches another person whether you realize it or not, every human being is important in the circle of life, you are important so go out and make a difference*

Closure

Remember on your journey there you will fail but that doesn't make you a failure. All leaders will have there weak moments, but the moments will pass. The cliché says, One can have a bad moment but does not have to have a bad day. Life is what you make it. Run your life like you want your business ran; either you're a hard worker, or always late and lazy.-(S. Green, 05/07) Everything in life is about choices and every choice has results.

There will be times that your expected outcome will not be established however that doesn't mean it's a negative. We are our own best friends and worst enemies end of the story. There are influences that make it easier or harder to make it but at the end of the day we choose our lives. For many people it is very difficult to see past the unavoidable reality of their life. However, no matter what odds are against you, you can overcome.

SHORT-TERM GOALS

SHORT-TERM GOALS

LONG-TERM GOALS

WRITTEN PLAN

WRITTEN PLAN

WRITTEN PLAN

BULLETED STEPS

BULLETED STEPS

DATES OF GOALS/ACTIONS

DATES OF GOALS/ACTIONS

DATES OF GOALS/ACTIONS

AFFIRMATIONS

- *REMEMEBR GOD IN EVERYTHING YOU DO*
- *YOU ARE SMART, BEAUTIFUL AND TALENTED*
- *BEAUTY IS ABOUT CHARACTER NOT ONLY THE PHYSICAL*
- *NOTHING CAN STOP YOUR SUCCESS BUT YOU*
- *EMBRACE THE JOY AND PAINS OF LIFE CHALLENGES*
- *LOVE YOURSELF AND OTHERS WILL DO THE SAME*
- *NEVER GIVE UP ON WHAT YOU BELIEVE*
- *YOU ARE UNIQUE AND SOMETIMES YOU HAVE TO SEARCH FOR YOUR HIDDEN TALENT*
- *YOU WILL ENJOY WHAT YOUR PURPOSED TO DO AND YOU WILL BE GOOD AT IT*

- *THE ONLY WAY TO NOT BECOMING A MILLIONAIRE IS IF THAT ISN'T TRULY YOUR GOAL OR GIVING UP*

AFFIRMATIONS

- *Remember being a millionaire is not only about money it's about true freedom*
- *You can have all the money in the world and no inner peace or happiness*
- *You have to be happy and content in your life*
- *Now go and be you at your best if you dare!*

About Me

March 26th 1982 a beautiful bright eye baby was born. That day the world would never be the same because a leader was born. I am twenty five years old woman, of Nigerian and Dominican descent. I am originally from Brooklyn New York. I was raised by my mother and step father. I have two brothers ages twenty six and twenty four. We are what you call stair-steppers. We are all a year apart from each other. My life has been filled with joys, but what seemed like routine obstacles. Despite the ebbs and flows of life I went away to college. I went away to Long Island University in Southampton NY, and my entire perspective of life altered in undergraduate. There were so many trees and beautiful sceneries. People would just say good afternoon upon making eye contact. I made a promise to myself to live a life with a better quality and obtain more lucrative means.

Then my last year of college September 28th 2003 I was in a tragic car accident and I ended up in a coma. The doctors said I would be paralyzed and brain dead. God gave me another chance in life. For those that do not believe in God the Lord Jesus that is your choice. This book is not about religion but freedom. Therefore, everyone has the freedom of choice and that's their right. Nonetheless, I am here for a reason. I know I am I am here to bring hope in the lives of millions of people that may not believe in themselves any more. As they are reading they no longer believe in good natured people. They may be jaded by the travesties in their life. I am here to say my life has not always been a walk in the park, yet I choose to never give up on myself. After the accident I went back to school for my masters. I am almost finished my MSED in Vocational Rehabilitation

Counseling. I choose to continue to live. I got married March 16th 2007(Marriage is a book in and of itself). I've always been strong minded and I've always felt like a fish out of water in many phases in my life. I just wasn't a conformist. My desire to tap into my individuality caused me discomfort at times because it isn't easy going against the masses. Once, one of my friends called me a black hippy. I smile now because I never thought of myself as a hippy. I have always naturally embraced peace and love not the pipe though. Every day is filled with hundreds of choices and thoughts. Basically, life will move no matter where we are in life. Time is one constant that no one can fight or change. I firmly believe one should not just be a drifter in life, or conform to "everyone's desires. Stay true to yourself, and stay consigned to your own happiness. That is what I did and my life has continued everyday to prove that and remember you are the master of your fate.